Sell Beyond Limits:

"Dominate Any Market and Achieve Unstoppable Growth"

Table of Contents

Foreword

- A Journey Beyond Limits: Unlocking Your Ultimate Potential
- Why This Book Will Transform Your Business and Your Life

Introduction

- The Game-Changer: Why Selling is Your Superpower
- How to Use This Playbook for Maximum Impact

Part 1: The Mindset of Limitless Success

Chapter 1: Think Beyond Limits

- Master the Billionaire Mindset
- The 4% Rule: How to Focus on What Moves the Money Needle

Chapter 2: Unlocking Relentless Drive

- Defeating the "Inner Critic" to Achieve Unstoppable Momentum
- Cultivating a Resilient and Winning Attitude

Part 2: The Foundations of Selling Like a Legend

Chapter 3: The Hero's Offer

- Crafting Irresistible Proposals That Customers Can't Refuse
- The Science of Creating Offers that Speak to the Heart

Chapter 4: Know Thy Buyer

- The Psychology of Understanding Your Dream Client
- Advanced Strategies for Pinpointing Buyer Pain Points

Part 3: Capturing Attention in a Noisy World

Chapter 5: The Digital Domination Toolkit

- Using AI, Social Media, and Automation to Generate Consistent Leads
- The 7 Traffic Channels You Must Master

Chapter 6: Magnetic Marketing

- Emotional Storytelling That Captivates Audiences
- Creating Viral Campaigns That Build Brand Loyalty

Part 4: Building Systems That Scale

Chapter 7: The Infinite Revenue Loop

- Automating Your Sales Funnel for Predictable Profits
- Scaling Without Losing the Human Touch

Chapter 8: Salesmanship Multiplied

- Turning Your Sales Message into a 24/7 Sales Machine
- How to Create High-Converting Ads and Content

Part 5: Driving Unstoppable Growth

Chapter 9: The Empathy Economy

- How to Build Trust and Connection for Long-Term Success
- Turning Clients into Raving Fans

Chapter 10: The Relentless Innovator

- Staying Ahead of Market Trends and Competitors
- Creating Blue Oceans in Any Industry

Part 6: Mastery and Beyond

Chapter 11: The Feedback Loop

- Analyzing and Optimizing Every Step of the Process
- Turning Failures Into Stepping Stones for Growth

Chapter 12: The Legacy of Limitless Success

- How to Build a Business that Outlasts You
- Empowering Others and Sending the Elevator Back Down

Chapter 13: The Network Effect

Building Powerful Connections That Multiply Your Success

- How to build and nurture a network of high-value relationships.
- The art of giving before receiving adding value to others.
- Leveraging your network to create business opportunities, collaborations, and growth.
- Real-life examples of how networks can amplify success.

Chapter 14: The Power of Personal Branding

Becoming the Face of Your Success

- Crafting a personal brand that aligns with your business goals.
- Using social media, content creation, and public speaking to establish authority.
- Building trust and relatability with your audience.
- Case studies of entrepreneurs who leveraged personal branding for exponential growth.

Chapter 15: Embracing AI and Future Technologies

Staying Ahead in a Rapidly Changing World

- How AI and automation are reshaping industries and opportunities.
- Practical ways to integrate AI into marketing, operations, and customer experience.
- Understanding blockchain, Web3, and other transformative technologies.
- Preparing for the future: anticipating and adapting to technological shifts.

Chapter 16: Mastering Emotional Intelligence

The Hidden Edge in Leadership and Business

- Why emotional intelligence (EQ) is more critical than ever.
- Understanding and managing your own emotions as an entrepreneur.

- Building empathy and strong relationships with your team, partners, and customers.
- Strategies to handle conflict, inspire loyalty, and lead with authenticity.

Chapter 17: The Global Entrepreneur

Expanding Your Business Beyond Borders

- Opportunities and challenges in international markets.
- Adapting your products, services, and messaging for different cultures.
- Navigating global regulations and logistics.
- Leveraging digital tools to reach customers worldwide.

Chapter 18: Resilience in the Face of Uncertainty

Thriving When the Unexpected Happens

- Strategies for navigating economic downturns, market shifts, and crises.
- The importance of a contingency plan and agile thinking.
- Turning adversity into opportunity: inspiring stories of businesses that thrived during challenging times.

Bonus: The Epic Case Studies

- Real Stories of Businesses That Went from Zero to Millions

Conclusion

- Your Next Chapter: A Call to Action for Limitless Growth

Foreword

A Journey Beyond Limits: Unlocking Your Ultimate Potential

Welcome to a journey that will redefine what you thought was possible—for your business, for your life, and for the legacy you are destined to create. This is more than a book; it's a declaration, a roadmap, and an unyielding call to action for those who dare to dream big and refuse to settle for mediocrity.

In a world bursting with noise and distractions, the difference between success and failure lies in clarity—clarity of purpose, clarity of action, and clarity of vision. This book is your compass, guiding you through the labyrinth of modern business to discover untapped opportunities, master the art of influence, and ultimately transform your life into one of unstoppable growth and abundance.

I believe in the power of human potential—your potential. Regardless of where you are starting from, this journey is about shattering limits and embracing the mindset of infinite possibility. It's about becoming the kind of person who doesn't just adapt to change but creates it. You are here because you have a fire within you, a hunger to achieve, and a relentless drive to make a difference. This book will fan that fire, sharpen your focus, and arm you with the tools to make your dreams a reality.

Why This Book Will Transform Your Business and Your Life

Let me be honest: this is not just another business book. This is not about vague theories or impractical advice. This is about actionable strategies, timeless principles, and a proven system that has helped countless entrepreneurs and business leaders build empires from scratch.

In the pages ahead, you will uncover the secrets to mastering the most critical skill in any business: selling. But selling here is not limited to transactions. It is about influence, persuasion, and creating value that makes people say, "Yes, this is exactly what I need." Whether you are selling a product, an idea, or your own vision of the future, this book will give you the keys to unlock the hearts and minds of your audience.

Here's why this book will transform you:

- **Clarity in Chaos**: You'll learn to cut through the noise of endless marketing gimmicks and focus on what truly works—principles that have stood the test of time and are adapted for today's digital age.
- **Unstoppable Systems**: You'll discover how to create repeatable, scalable systems that not only generate consistent revenue but free you from the hamster wheel of day-to-day firefighting.
- **Mindset Shift**: You'll gain a new perspective on what it means to succeed, adopting the mindset of limitless potential and learning to think like the top 1% of achievers.
- **Actionable Steps**: Each chapter is designed to move you forward, with practical exercises and tools that ensure you're not just reading but implementing and growing.

This book is your invitation to rise above the ordinary and join the ranks of extraordinary achievers. But remember, transformation doesn't happen by chance; it happens by choice. The tools, insights, and strategies are here, waiting for you to take them and put them to work. It's your turn to embrace the journey, unlock your ultimate potential, and rewrite your story of success.

So, are you ready? Let's begin. Together, we'll forge a path to greatness that you never thought possible.

Sincerely,
Chad T
Author of "Sell Beyond Limits"

Introduction

The Game-Changer: Why Selling is Your Superpower

Selling is not just a skill—it's a superpower. Whether you realize it or not, your ability to sell can shape the trajectory of your life and business in ways you've never imagined. Yet, when people hear the word "selling," it often conjures up images of pushy salespeople or cheap gimmicks. Let me tell you something: that's not selling. True selling is an art, a science, and a life-changing force.

At its core, selling is about influence—the ability to inspire action, create desire, and solve problems. It's about building trust, communicating value, and creating lasting relationships. And here's the best part: selling is not just for seasoned business veterans or extroverted go-getters. Selling is for anyone willing to master the craft.

Imagine a world where:

- You can present your ideas with such clarity and passion that people rally behind your vision.
- Your business generates a consistent, predictable flow of customers who are eager to buy from you.
- You wake up every day knowing that you have the power to create opportunities, open doors, and change lives.

This is what selling can do for you. It's the ultimate equalizer. No matter your background, education, or starting point, selling levels the playing field and equips you with the tools to achieve extraordinary success.

The strategies in this book will teach you to harness this superpower, turning it into a force that not only drives revenue but transforms your life. Selling isn't just something you do—it's a mindset, a skillset, and, ultimately, a lifestyle.

How to Use This Playbook for Maximum Impact

This is not a book you simply read and put back on the shelf. This is a playbook designed for action, growth, and results. Every chapter is packed with practical strategies, real-world examples, and actionable steps that you can implement immediately.

Here's how to get the most out of this playbook:

1. **Commit to the Process** This book is a journey, and like any journey, it requires dedication and focus. Be prepared to dig deep, challenge your assumptions, and step outside your comfort zone. Selling mastery doesn't happen overnight, but with consistent effort, the transformation will be undeniable.
2. **Take Notes and Reflect** Highlight passages, jot down ideas, and reflect on how each concept applies to your business and life. The more engaged you are, the more you'll extract from these pages.
3. **Complete the Action Steps** At the end of every chapter, you'll find actionable steps designed to put theory into practice. Don't skip these. Implementation is the bridge between knowledge and results.
4. **Leverage the Tools** Throughout the book, you'll find worksheets, templates, and exercises. These are your accelerators. Use them to organize your thoughts, craft your strategies, and track your progress.
5. **Join the Community** Selling is a collaborative effort. Connect with like-minded individuals, share your experiences, and learn from others. The "Sell Beyond Limits" community is here to support you every step of the way.
6. **Review and Revisit** The principles in this book are timeless. As your business grows and evolves, come back to these strategies to refine and adapt them to new challenges. What works today will work even better tomorrow when you revisit it with experience and insight.

This book is your blueprint to unlock your selling superpower and create the life and business you've always dreamed of. The only question now is: are you ready to take the first step? If your answer is yes, then let's dive in and make it happen.

Chapter 1: Think Beyond Limits

Master the Billionaire Mindset

Success begins in the mind. If you want to achieve extraordinary results, you must think differently than the average person. The truth is every billionaire—self-made or otherwise—shares one common trait: they think on a level far beyond the ordinary. They approach challenges, opportunities, and even failures with a mindset rooted in abundance, resilience, and strategy.

To master the billionaire mindset, you need to understand their approach to three critical elements:

1. **Time as the Ultimate Asset** Billionaires understand that time is their most valuable and non-renewable resource. They don't squander it on low-priority tasks. Instead, they focus on activities that yield exponential returns—strategizing, innovating, and building relationships. Every minute is invested purposefully.

    Ask yourself: Are you spending your time on tasks that truly matter? Or are you caught up in the trivial and urgent?

2. **Resilience in the Face of Failure** Failure is not an endpoint; it's a stepping stone. Billionaires don't fear failure; they embrace it as a necessary part of growth. They learn from their mistakes and use those lessons to pivot and improve.

    Adopt this mindset: Every setback is a setup for a comeback. How can you turn your challenges into opportunities for growth?

3. **Relentless Focus on Value Creation** Billionaires don't just chase profits; they create value that transforms lives. Whether it's a product, service, or idea, their focus is on solving problems and meeting needs better than anyone else.

    Consider this: What unique value can you offer that sets you apart in your market?

The billionaire mindset is not a trait you're born with. It's a way of thinking that you can cultivate with intention and practice. By adopting these principles, you'll start to see opportunities where others see obstacles and think at a level that propels you toward limitless success.

The 4% Rule: How to Focus on What Moves the Money Needle

Not all tasks are created equally. In fact, the majority of what we do in business has little impact on our results. The key to skyrocketing your success lies in identifying and focusing on the 4% of activities that drive 64% of your results. This is an evolution of the famed Pareto Principle (80/20 rule) and is the ultimate guide for maximizing your impact.

Identifying Your 4%

To find your 4%, ask yourself these questions:

- What tasks generate the most revenue for my business?
- Which activities have the greatest long-term impact on my goals?
- What actions produce exponential results compared to their effort?

Examples of high-leverage 4% activities include:

- Crafting compelling offers and sales strategies
- Building and nurturing relationships with high-value clients
- Creating systems that automate and scale your business
- Developing new products or services that meet market demands

Eliminating or Delegating the 96%

The other 96% of activities still need to get done, but not by you. These might include administrative tasks, email management, or routine customer service. Delegate, outsource, or automate these to free yourself for the work that truly matters.

Designing Your Day Around the 4%

Once you've identified your 4%, structure your day to prioritize these tasks:

1. **Morning Deep Work**: Begin your day with uninterrupted focus on your most critical activities. These are the tasks that align with your 4%.
2. **Batch Low-Value Tasks**: Allocate a specific time for lower-priority tasks and tackle them in batches.
3. **Reflect and Optimize**: At the end of each day, evaluate how much time you spent on your 4%. Adjust your approach to ensure maximum alignment with your goals.

The Compounding Effect

When you consistently invest your time in the 4%, the results compound. Over weeks, months, and years, this laser focus will set you apart from your competitors and position you as a leader in your field.

Action Steps:

1. List all your current activities and categorize them into high-value (4%) and low-value (96%).
2. Create a plan to delegate or eliminate the 96%.
3. Develop a daily schedule that prioritizes your 4% and protects that time fiercely.
4. Review your progress weekly and refine your focus.

Thinking beyond limits and mastering the 4% rule will not only transform your business but also redefine how you approach success. The journey to limitless success begins now—and it begins with you.

Chapter 2: Unlocking Relentless Drive

Defeating the "Inner Critic" to Achieve Unstoppable Momentum

Inside every ambitious individual lies a voice that questions, doubts, and undermines. It's the "Inner Critic," and left unchecked, it can derail even the most talented and driven people. If you want to achieve relentless drive, you must not only silence this voice but turn it into a motivator for action.

Understanding the Inner Critic

The Inner Critic stems from fear: fear of failure, rejection, or not being good enough. It whispers thoughts like, *"What if I'm not ready?"* or *"Others are more qualified than I am."* These doubts are natural, but they're not facts. The Inner Critic thrives on hesitation and feeds on your insecurities.

Strategies to Defeat the Inner Critic

1. **Identify the Voice**: Recognize when the Inner Critic is speaking. Journaling or mindfulness can help you pinpoint its triggers.
2. **Reframe the Dialogue**: Replace negative self-talk with empowering affirmations. For example:
   o Inner Critic: *"You can't handle this challenge."
   o Reframe: *"This challenge is my opportunity to grow and excel."
3. **Take Immediate Action**: Action is the antidote to doubt. Break tasks into small, manageable steps and start immediately. The faster you act, the less power the Inner Critic holds.
4. **Celebrate Small Wins**: Acknowledge every step forward, no matter how small. Momentum builds when you focus on progress, not perfection.
5. **Surround Yourself with Encouragement**: Seek out mentors, supportive friends, or inspiring content. Positive reinforcement drowns out self-doubt and reinforces belief in your abilities.

The Inner Critic is not your enemy—it's a challenge to overcome. Each time you push past its doubts, you grow stronger, more confident, and more capable of achieving greatness.

Cultivating a Resilient and Winning Attitude

Relentless drive requires more than ambition; it demands resilience. A winning attitude is forged in the crucible of challenges and setbacks. The good news? Resilience can be cultivated like any other skill.

The Pillars of Resilience

1. **Embrace Challenges**: See obstacles not as roadblocks but as stepping stones. Every challenge carries a lesson that prepares you for greater success.
2. **Focus on Your Why**: When the journey gets tough, your purpose becomes your anchor. Why did you start? What's at stake if you quit? Reconnect with your vision to fuel your persistence.
3. **Practice Gratitude**: Gratitude shifts your focus from what's wrong to what's right. Daily reflection on your wins, strengths, and opportunities builds a positive outlook.
4. **Develop Emotional Agility**: Resilient people don't avoid emotions; they manage them. Learn to acknowledge stress, fear, or disappointment without letting them dictate your actions.
5. **Commit to Continuous Growth**: Adopt a learner's mindset. Failure isn't the opposite of success—it's part of the process. Every misstep is an opportunity to refine your approach and grow stronger.

Building a Winning Attitude

1. **Visualize Success**: Begin each day by envisioning your goals as already achieved. This primes your mind for success and aligns your actions with your aspirations.
2. **Adopt a Problem-Solving Mindset**: When problems arise, ask: *"What can I do to overcome this?"* Rather than dwelling on the issue, focus on actionable solutions.
3. **Stay Consistent**: Drive isn't about intensity; it's about consistency. Even on days when motivation wanes, show up and put in the work.

Small, consistent actions yield monumental results over time.

4. **Lead with Positivity**: Positivity isn't naive; it's a strategy. Optimism fuels creativity, strengthens relationships, and keeps you moving forward.
5. **Learn to Rest, Not Quit**: Burnout is the enemy of drive. Listen to your body and mind. Rest when needed, but never confuse rest with giving up.

Action Steps:

1. Write down three instances when your Inner Critic held you back and reframe them with empowering statements.
2. Identify one current challenge and list three actionable steps you can take to overcome it.
3. Create a morning ritual that includes gratitude, visualization, and affirmations to prime your mindset for success.
4. Commit to showing up every day for the next 30 days, even when motivation is low. Track your progress and celebrate each win.

When you defeat the Inner Critic and cultivate resilience, you unlock the relentless drive needed to achieve unstoppable momentum. With this chapter as your guide, you're ready to conquer self-doubt and seize every opportunity that lies ahead.

Part 2: The Foundations of Selling Like a Legend

Chapter 3: The Hero's Offer

Crafting Irresistible Proposals That Customers Can't Refuse

At the heart of every successful business lies a hero-worthy offer—one so compelling, so irresistible, that customers feel compelled to say yes. This chapter is about transforming your offers from ordinary to extraordinary. It's about creating value so clear and impactful that it transcends price objections, competition, and even customer hesitation.

An irresistible offer does more than sell a product or service; it inspires trust, triggers emotional engagement, and positions your brand as the solution to your customers' deepest needs.

The Anatomy of an Irresistible Offer

1. **Laser-Focused Clarity**: A confused customer never buys. Your offer should clearly state what's included, the benefits, and the results your customer can expect. Avoid jargon and complexity.

   Example: Instead of saying, *"Our software enhances productivity,"* say, *"Our software saves you 10 hours per week by automating your scheduling and task management."

2. **Solve a Burning Problem**: The best offers address your customer's most urgent pain points. Identify the problems that keep them up at night and position your offer as the perfect solution.

   Ask Yourself: What is the #1 challenge my ideal customer faces, and how does my offer provide the ultimate relief?

3. **Promise Transformational Results**: Your offer should highlight the transformation your customer will experience. Focus on outcomes, not just features.

   Example: "Lose 15 pounds in 30 days without giving up your favorite foods."

4. **Add Scarcity or Urgency**: People are naturally inclined to act when there's a sense of urgency or limited availability.

   Example: "Only 50 spots available—enroll by Friday to lock in your discount."

5. **Eliminate Risk**: Mitigate hesitation by offering a strong guarantee or risk-reversal. This builds trust and confidence.

Example: "If you're not thrilled with your results within 30 days, we'll refund every penny—no questions asked."

The Science of Creating Offers that Speak to the Heart

Humans make decisions based on emotions first and justify them with logic later. To craft offers that resonate deeply, you must connect with your customers on an emotional level.

The Emotional Triggers Behind Every Great Offer

1. **Desire**: Tap into what your customers want most: freedom, security, love, recognition, or status. Build your offer around fulfilling these desires.

    Example: A luxury watch isn't about telling time; it's about signaling success.

2. **Fear**: Highlight what your customers stand to lose if they don't act. Fear of missing out (FOMO), losing money, or being left behind can be powerful motivators.

    Example: "Without this insurance, a single accident could wipe out your savings."

3. **Belonging**: People crave connection and community. Position your offer as a way for customers to join a movement or tribe.

    Example: "Join thousands of entrepreneurs who've already transformed their businesses with our system."

4. **Hope**: Show your customers what's possible. Paint a vivid picture of the brighter future they can achieve with your help.

Example: "Imagine waking up every day with boundless energy and confidence in your body."

Crafting Your Hero's Offer: A Step-by-Step Framework

1. **Identify Your Dream Customer**:
   o Who are they?
   o What do they need?
   o What are their pain points?
2. **Define the Core Value**:
   o What specific transformation does your offer deliver?
   o How does it improve their life or solve their problem?
3. **Bundle Irresistible Bonuses**:
   o Add high-value extras that amplify the appeal of your main offer.
   o **Example**: "Sign up today and get access to our exclusive productivity masterclass ($499 value) for free."
4. **Create a Strong Call to Action**:
   o Be direct and clear about what you want your customers to do.
   o **Example**: "Click the button below to start your journey to financial freedom today."
5. **Test, Refine, Repeat**:
   o Continuously test different versions of your offer.
   o Experiment with headlines, pricing, guarantees, and urgency.

Action Steps:

1. Write down the top three problems your customers face and brainstorm how your offer solves each.
2. Craft a transformation statement for your offer: *"With [my product/service], you'll go from [current state] to [desired state] in [timeframe]."
3. Add at least one element of scarcity or urgency to your current offers.
4. Revisit your guarantees. Ask yourself: *"How can I eliminate even more risk for my customer?"

Your hero's offer is more than just a pitch; it's a promise. When you craft it with care and precision, you're not just selling a product—you're changing lives.

Chapter 4: Know Thy Buyer

The Psychology of Understanding Your Dream Client

The key to building an unstoppable business lies in one simple truth: if you don't know your buyers, you can't sell to them effectively. Truly understanding your dream client—their desires, fears, habits, and decision-making processes—is what separates average businesses from market leaders.

Your buyer isn't just a demographic or a statistic; they are a living, breathing person with unique needs and motivations. The more deeply you understand them, the better you can position your products or services as the perfect solution to their problems.

The Buyer's Journey

Every customer embarks on a journey before they make a purchase. This journey typically has three stages:

1. **Awareness**:
   - The buyer realizes they have a problem or need.
   - Your role: Educate and inform them about their challenges.
2. **Consideration**:
   - The buyer actively seeks solutions and evaluates options.
   - Your role: Showcase how your offer stands out and aligns with their needs.
3. **Decision**:
   - The buyer chooses the solution they believe will deliver the best results.
   - Your role: Make it easy for them to say "yes" with clear benefits, testimonials, and a compelling call to action.

Understanding where your buyer is in this journey allows you to tailor your messaging and approach for maximum impact.

Advanced Strategies for Pinpointing Buyer Pain Points

Pain points are the problems, challenges, or frustrations your customers face. When you can pinpoint these with precision, you become their trusted solution provider. Here's how to uncover and leverage these insights:

1. Conduct Deep Research

- **Surveys and Interviews**: Directly ask your customers about their biggest challenges. Questions like, *"What's the hardest part of [specific area]?"* or *"What's holding you back from achieving [specific goal]?"* can reveal valuable insights.
- **Analyze Competitor Reviews**: Dive into reviews of similar products or services to discover what buyers love and what frustrates them. This is a goldmine for understanding gaps in the market.
- **Monitor Social Media Conversations**: Platforms like Facebook groups, Reddit, and Twitter often host unfiltered discussions where buyers share their pain points.

2. Use Empathy Mapping

An empathy map helps you step into your buyer's shoes. Consider these four quadrants:

- **Think and Feel**: What are their fears, hopes, and dreams?
- **See**: What are they exposed to daily (ads, competitors, peers)?
- **Say and Do**: How do they describe their challenges? What actions are they taking?
- **Hear**: What advice or feedback are they receiving from others?

This exercise gives you a 360-degree view of your buyer's world.

3. Identify Emotional and Functional Needs

Buyers have two layers of needs:

- **Functional Needs**: The practical, logical problem your product solves. (*"I need software that organizes my tasks.")

- **Emotional Needs**: The deeper, often unspoken desires tied to their identity or feelings. (*"I want to feel in control and accomplished.")

Positioning your offer to meet both needs creates a compelling reason to buy.

4. Uncover Their Barriers

Ask yourself: What might prevent this person from buying? Common barriers include:

- **Time**: Do they believe your solution will save them time or require too much effort?
- **Cost**: Do they see your product as an investment or an expense?
- **Skepticism**: Do they trust that your product will deliver results?

Address these concerns proactively in your messaging.

Crafting Your Buyer Persona

A buyer persona is a detailed profile of your ideal customer. Use the following template to define your dream client:

- **Demographics**:
  - Age, gender, income, location, education level.
- **Psychographics**:
  - Goals, values, lifestyle, hobbies.
- **Pain Points**:
  - Specific challenges or frustrations they're facing.
- **Buying Behaviors**:
  - Where do they shop? How do they make decisions? Who influences them?

- **Preferred Channels**:
  - Do they consume information on Instagram, LinkedIn, email newsletters, or podcasts?

Example Persona: *"Sarah is a 35-year-old entrepreneur who struggles with time management while scaling her business. She values efficiency, uses productivity tools, and follows thought leaders on LinkedIn. She needs a simple yet effective solution to manage her daily tasks and free up time for strategic planning."*

Action Steps:

1. Research your audience using surveys, interviews, and social media.
2. Create an empathy map for your dream client.
3. Write a detailed buyer persona using the template above.
4. Review your current offers and messaging. Do they align with your customer's pain points and desires?

By understanding the psychology of your dream client and pinpointing their pain points, you can craft offers and messaging that resonate deeply, leading to stronger connections, higher conversions, and long-term loyalty. Know thy buyer, and success will follow.

Chapter 5: The Digital Domination Toolkit

Using AI, Social Media, and Automation to Generate Consistent Leads

In today's digital-first world, the businesses that thrive are those that embrace cutting-edge tools and strategies to connect with their audience.

From AI-driven insights to automation that works while you sleep, the potential to dominate your market has never been greater.

This chapter will equip you with the ultimate toolkit to generate consistent leads and grow your business. By mastering AI, social media, and automation, you'll build a system that scales your efforts while maintaining a personal touch.

Leveraging AI for Insights and Personalization

1. **Audience Analysis**: Use AI tools like Google Analytics, HubSpot, or SEMrush to analyze customer behavior, identify trends, and predict future needs. AI uncovers patterns that help you refine your messaging and offerings.
2. **Personalized Marketing**: AI-driven platforms like ChatGPT, Jasper, or Adobe Sensei allow you to create personalized email campaigns, social media posts, and even product recommendations tailored to individual preferences.
3. **Chatbots and Customer Support**: AI chatbots like Intercom or Drift ensure 24/7 customer interaction, answering common queries, and guiding prospects further down the sales funnel.
4. **Content Generation**: Tools like Grammarly, Canva, or Copy smith use AI to enhance your content creation, from social posts to blog articles, ensuring high-quality outputs in record time.

Dominating Social Media

Social media platforms are powerful channels for building your brand, engaging with your audience, and generating leads. Here's how to dominate:

1. **Choose the Right Platforms**: Focus on platforms where your target audience is most active. For B2B, LinkedIn is invaluable. For younger audiences, Instagram or TikTok might be ideal.
2. **Create Shareable Content**:
    - Focus on value: tips, insights, and behind-the-scenes content.
    - Leverage visuals: videos, infographics, and memes drive engagement.
    - Use storytelling: connect emotionally with your audience.
3. **Engage Consistently**: Social media is not a "set it and forget it" tool. Reply to comments, share user-generated content, and participate in conversations to build community.
4. **Social Listening**: Tools like Hootsuite or Brand24 help you monitor mentions of your brand or industry, allowing you to respond proactively to opportunities and challenges.
5. **Paid Advertising**: Amplify your reach with paid campaigns. Platforms like Facebook Ads Manager or Google Ads allow hyper-targeted ads based on demographics, interests, and behaviors.

Automating Lead Generation

1. **Email Automation**: Platforms like Mailchimp, Active Campaign, or Convert Kit allow you to create automated workflows that nurture leads through personalized drip campaigns.
2. **CRM Integration**: A robust CRM like Salesforce or Zoho automates lead tracking, scoring, and follow-up, ensuring no opportunity slips through the cracks.
3. **Retargeting Campaigns**: Retarget visitors who didn't convert with personalized ads through Google or Facebook. Automation ensures they see your offer multiple times, increasing the likelihood of conversion.

4. **Landing Pages and Funnels**: Use tools like Click Funnels, Lead pages, or Un bounce to create high-converting landing pages and sales funnels that automate the customer journey.

The 7 Traffic Channels You Must Master

1. **Search Engine Optimization (SEO)**:
   - Optimize your website and content for keywords your audience searches for.
   - Focus on building backlinks and creating high-quality, shareable content.
2. **Pay-Per-Click Advertising (PPC)**:
   - Use Google Ads or Bing Ads for targeted keyword campaigns.
   - Test ad copy and landing pages to maximize ROI.
3. **Content Marketing**:
   - Regularly publish blogs, videos, and downloadable resources that educate and engage your audience.
   - Position yourself as an authority in your field.
4. **Social Media Marketing**:
   - Build a strong presence on platforms your audience frequents.
   - Engage with followers and post consistently.
5. **Affiliate Marketing**:
   - Partner with influencers or businesses to promote your offerings.
   - Provide incentives like commissions or exclusive discounts.
6. **Email Marketing**:
   - Build a strong email list and nurture it with valuable content.
   - Segment your audience for tailored campaigns.
7. **Referral Traffic**:
   - Leverage partnerships, guest blogging, and influencer collaborations to drive traffic from trusted sources.

Action Steps:

1. Identify which traffic channels align best with your target audience.
2. Choose one AI tool and implement it in your marketing workflow.
3. Create or update your social media strategy to prioritize engagement and consistency.
4. Build one automated email sequence to nurture leads.
5. Optimize a landing page for one of your offers, focusing on clarity and conversion.

By integrating AI, social media, and automation with the mastery of these seven traffic channels, you'll create a lead-generation engine that never sleeps. Digital domination isn't just a goal—it's the future of business.

Chapter 6: Magnetic Marketing

Emotional Storytelling That Captivates Audiences

Stories have the power to move mountains—and markets. At the heart of magnetic marketing lies the ability to tell stories that resonate so deeply, they capture attention, inspire action, and create lasting loyalty. Emotional storytelling bridges the gap between your brand and your audience, turning casual observers into loyal advocates.

The Power of Emotion in Storytelling

People buy with their hearts and justify with their heads. To captivate your audience:

1. **Tap into Core Emotions**:
   - Happiness: Inspire joy with success stories or uplifting outcomes.
   - Fear: Highlight what's at stake if action isn't taken.
   - Hope: Paint a picture of a better, brighter future.
   - Belonging: Create a sense of community and shared purpose.
2. **Make It Relatable**: Your audience should see themselves in your story. Speak their language, mirror their struggles, and celebrate their dreams.
3. **Focus on Transformation**: Every great story has a hero— and that hero is your audience. Show how your product or service can guide them from their current pain to their desired success.

Crafting Your Brand's Story

1. **Define the Hero**: Identify your ideal customer and their challenges. What keeps them up at night? What do they aspire to?
2. **Show the Struggle**: Highlight the problem your audience faces. Use vivid descriptions to make it real and relatable.
3. **Present the Solution**: Position your brand, product, or service as the guide or tool that helps them overcome their challenges.
4. **Celebrate the Outcome**: End your story with the triumph—a clear, compelling vision of what life looks like after solving the problem.

Storytelling in Action

- **Case Studies**: Share real-life transformations from your customers.
- **Origin Stories**: Highlight your journey and the "why" behind your brand.
- **Behind-the-Scenes**: Offer a peek into the human side of your business.

Creating Viral Campaigns That Build Brand Loyalty

Viral campaigns don't just happen; they're engineered. By combining creativity, strategy, and emotional resonance, you can create content that spreads like wildfire while reinforcing your brand's message.

The Ingredients of a Viral Campaign

1. **Emotionally Charged Content**: Content that evokes strong emotions is more likely to be shared. Whether it's humor, inspiration, or outrage, tap into feelings that drive action.
2. **A Clear, Shareable Message**: Simplify your message so it's easy to understand and share. Clarity amplifies reach.
3. **Timeliness**: Ride the wave of trending topics, events, or cultural moments. Timely campaigns capture attention in the moment.
4. **Incentivize Sharing**: Give your audience a reason to spread the word. Contests, giveaways, or the promise of recognition can motivate participation.
5. **Leverage User-Generated Content**: Encourage your audience to create and share their own content tied to your campaign. This builds authenticity and expands your reach.

Steps to Build a Viral Campaign

1. **Set a Clear Objective**: What do you want to achieve? Increased brand awareness, lead generation, or a spike in sales?
2. **Know Your Audience**: Tailor your content to the preferences, humor, and values of your target demographic.
3. **Choose the Right Platforms**: Viral content needs a stage. Use platforms where your audience is most active and likely to engage.
4. **Create a Memorable Hook**: Whether it's a catchy tagline, a surprising twist, or an iconic visual, make sure your campaign has a standout element.
5. **Measure and Adapt**: Track the performance of your campaign and be ready to pivot if needed. Monitor shares, comments, and conversions to gauge success.

Building Brand Loyalty Through Campaigns

Loyalty isn't built in a day, but viral campaigns can lay a strong foundation. Here's how to convert viral moments into lasting relationships:

1. **Engage Continuously**: Respond to comments, thank sharers, and interact with your audience. Building rapport fosters loyalty.
2. **Reward Participation**: Recognize and reward your most engaged followers. Whether it's a shoutout or exclusive perks, appreciation goes a long way.
3. **Reinforce Your Values**: Viral campaigns should align with your brand's core values. This consistency builds trust and connection.
4. **Follow Up**: After a successful campaign, nurture your new audience with meaningful content, offers, or invitations to join your community.

Action Steps:

1. Craft a 3-minute brand story that highlights your audience as the hero.
2. Brainstorm a viral campaign idea tied to an upcoming event, trend, or cultural moment.
3. Plan a follow-up strategy to engage and nurture new followers gained from the campaign.
4. Create a checklist for emotional resonance in all your marketing efforts.

By mastering emotional storytelling and designing campaigns that resonate, you'll not only capture attention but also create a loyal following. Magnetic marketing turns customers into advocates, ensuring your brand remains unforgettable.

Part 4: Building Systems That Scale

Chapter 7: The Infinite Revenue Loop

Automating Your Sales Funnel for Predictable Profits

In the world of business, predictability equals power. An automated sales funnel ensures that your business runs like a well-oiled machine, continuously attracting, converting, and nurturing leads without requiring constant manual input.

This is the Infinite Revenue Loop—a system designed to generate consistent profits while freeing you to focus on growth and innovation.

Understanding the Sales Funnel

A sales funnel is the journey your customers take from awareness to purchase. An automated funnel uses technology to guide prospects through this process, delivering the right message at the right time to maximize conversions.

The Funnel Stages:

1. **Awareness:** Attracting potential customers who discover your brand for the first time.
2. **Consideration:** Nurturing leads with valuable content and building trust.
3. **Decision:** Converting leads into paying customers.
4. **Retention:** Keeping customers engaged and encouraging repeat purchases.
5. **Advocacy:** Turning satisfied customers into brand ambassadors.

Building an Automated Sales Funnel

1. **Attract Leads:**
   - **Content Marketing:** Publish blogs, videos, or social posts that educate and entertain.
   - **Lead Magnets:** Offer free resources like eBooks, templates, or webinars in exchange for email addresses.
   - **SEO and Ads:** Optimize your website for search engines and run targeted ad campaigns to drive traffic.
2. **Capture Information:**
   - Use landing pages with compelling offers to collect contact information. Tools like Click Funnels or Lead pages can help streamline this process.

- o Ensure your forms are simple and user-friendly, asking only for essential details.
3. **Nurture Leads:**
   - o Set up email sequences to educate and build trust. Platforms like Mailchimp or Active Campaign make this easy.
   - o Use AI-driven tools to personalize emails based on user behavior.
   - o Share case studies, testimonials, or behind-the-scenes content to establish credibility.
4. **Convert Leads:**
   - o Create high-converting sales pages with clear calls to action.
   - o Use scarcity and urgency to drive immediate action (e.g., limited time offers or bonuses).
   - o Incorporate retargeting ads to re-engage visitors who didn't convert initially.
5. **Delight and Upsell:**
   - o Send personalized thank-you messages after purchases.
   - o Offer upsells or cross-sells for complementary products or services.
   - o Use surveys to gather feedback and improve your customer experience.
6. **Automate Follow-Ups:**
   - o Automated follow-up emails to encourage repeat purchases or referrals.
   - o Use chatbots or SMS marketing for timely, personalized communications.

Scaling Without Losing the Human Touch

As your business grows, maintaining a personal connection with your audience becomes increasingly challenging. However, automation doesn't mean sacrificing authenticity. With the right strategies, you can scale while keeping the human touch.

Strategies to Maintain Authenticity

1. **Segment Your Audience:** Divide your audience into groups based on behavior, demographics, or preferences. Tailor your messaging to each segment to ensure relevance.
2. **Use Personalized Automation:**
   - Address recipients by name and reference their actions (e.g., "We noticed you downloaded our guide…").
   - Tools like ActiveCampaign or HubSpot enable advanced personalization at scale.
3. **Engage Through Video:**
   - Use personalized video messages in your email sequences to create a stronger connection.
   - Platforms like Bonjoro or Loom make this easy and scalable.
4. **Leverage Social Proof:**
   - Highlight customer reviews, success stories, and user-generated content.
   - Authentic testimonials resonate more than generic marketing claims.
5. **Be Available:**
   - Use chatbots for instant responses but ensure there's an easy way to escalate to a human when needed.
   - Offer live Q&A sessions or webinars to interact directly with your audience.

Automate Feedback and Improvement

Scaling is an ongoing process of refinement. Use automation to:

- **Gather Feedback:** Send automated surveys post-purchase to understand customer satisfaction.
- **Analyze Data:** Use AI tools to identify patterns and areas for improvement.
- **Implement Updates:** Continuously optimize your funnel based on insights and feedback.

The Compounding Effect of the Infinite Revenue Loop

The beauty of the Infinite Revenue Loop is its compounding nature. Each stage of the funnel feeds into the next, creating a self-sustaining system that:

- Reduces lead acquisition costs over time.
- Increases customer lifetime value (CLV).
- Enhances brand loyalty and advocacy.

Action Steps:

1. Map out your current sales funnel and identify gaps or inefficiencies.
2. Choose a platform to automate your funnel's key stages (e.g., email marketing, landing pages, or chatbots).
3. Create a segmentation strategy to personalize your communication.
4. Test and optimize each stage of your funnel to improve conversions.
5. Set up feedback loops to ensure continuous improvement.

By automating your sales funnel and scaling with care, you can unlock predictable profits while preserving the human touch that makes your brand unique. The Infinite Revenue Loop isn't just a system; it's a strategy for sustained, scalable success.

Chapter 8: Salesmanship Multiplied

Turning Your Sales Message into a 24/7 Sales Machine

Great salesmanship isn't confined to in-person meetings or phone calls. In today's digital landscape, your sales message can work for you around the clock, reaching potential customers anytime, anywhere. By mastering the art of scalable sales messaging, you can create a system that continuously converts prospects into buyers without you being present.

The Core Principles of Scalable Sales Messaging

1. **Clarity Above All**: Your sales message must be simple, direct, and easy to understand. A confused prospect never buys.

   Example: Replace complex jargon like, "Our solution utilizes cutting-edge AI algorithms to optimize your workflow," with, "Our software saves you 10 hours a week by automating repetitive tasks."

2. **Speak to Pain Points**: Highlight the problems your audience faces and show how your product or service solves them.

   Formula: *Problem + Solution + Benefit* = Irresistible Sales Message

3. **Create a Sense of Urgency**: Use time-sensitive language or limited offers to encourage immediate action.

   Example: "Sign up today and get 50% off—offer ends at midnight!"

4. **Social Proof Builds Trust**: Incorporate testimonials, case studies, or user reviews to validate your claims.

   Example: "Join 10,000+ happy customers who've doubled their productivity with our tool."

5. **Strong Calls to Action (CTAs)**: Your CTA should be specific and action oriented.

   Example: Instead of "Learn More," use "Get Started Today" or "Claim Your Free Trial."

How to Create High-Converting Ads and Content

Your ads and content are your 24/7 sales representatives. To maximize their impact, you need to combine persuasive copy, compelling visuals, and strategic targeting.

Step 1: Write Persuasive Copy

1. **Start with an Attention-Grabbing Hook**:
   - Use a bold statement, question, or intriguing fact.
   - **Example**: "Struggling to grow your business? Here's the secret top entrepreneurs don't want you to know…"

2. **Focus on Benefits Over Features**:
   - Highlight what your audience gains, not just what your product does.
   - **Example**: Instead of "Our software has advanced analytics," say, "Get insights that double your ROI in half the time."

3. **Create an Emotional Connection**:
   - Use stories or scenarios that resonate with your audience.
   - **Example**: "Imagine never worrying about where your next lead is coming from…"

4. **Include a Clear CTA**:
   - End with a strong directive that tells the prospect exactly what to do next.
   - **Example**: "Click below to schedule your free consultation now."

Step 2: Design Visually Compelling Ads

1. **Use High-Quality Images or Videos**:
   - Eye-catching visuals increase engagement.
   - Ensure visuals align with your brand identity.
2. **Highlight Key Messages Visually**:
   - Use bold text overlays to emphasize benefits or offers.
   - **Example**: "Save 50% Today" or "Risk-Free for 30 Days."
3. **Keep Layouts Clean and Focused**:
   - Avoid clutter. Stick to one primary message per ad.

Step 3: Target Strategically

1. **Leverage Audience Data**:
   - Use tools like Facebook Ads Manager or Google Analytics to understand your audience's demographics, interests, and behaviors.
2. **Segment Your Campaigns**:
   - Create separate ads for different audience segments, such as first-time visitors versus returning customers.
3. **Use Retargeting**:
   - Re-engage users who visited your website but didn't convert with personalized ads.

Step 4: Optimize for Performance

1. **A/B Test Everything**:
   - Test headlines, visuals, CTAs, and offers to identify what resonates most.
2. **Analyze Metrics**:
   - Track click-through rates (CTR), conversion rates, and cost per acquisition (CPA) to measure success.
3. **Iterate and Improve**:
   - Use insights from your data to refine your ads and content over time.

Scaling Your Sales Machine

1. **Create Evergreen Content**: Develop blog posts, videos, or lead magnets that remain relevant and continue to attract leads long after they're published.
2. **Automate Your Ad Campaigns**: Platforms like Google Ads and Facebook allow you to set up automated bidding strategies to maximize ROI.
3. **Repurpose Content Across Channels**: Turn a high-performing blog post into a video, infographic, and social media post to reach broader audiences.
4. **Monitor and Adapt**: Stay agile. Consumer preferences change, and so should your campaigns. Regularly review performance and pivot as needed.

Action Steps:

1. Write a 3-sentence sales message that highlights your audience's problem, your solution, and a key benefit.
2. Create one high-converting ad using the principles outlined above.
3. Identify one piece of existing content to repurpose across multiple platforms.
4. Set up a retargeting campaign to re-engage website visitors.

By turning your sales message into a 24/7 machine and creating high-converting ads and content, you'll build a scalable system that works tirelessly to grow your business. Salesmanship multiplied isn't just a strategy—it's your competitive edge.

Chapter 9: The Empathy Economy

How to Build Trust and Connection for Long-Term Success

In today's business landscape, success is no longer defined solely by profit margins or market dominance. It's about connection, trust, and the ability to foster authentic relationships with your audience.

Welcome to the empathy economy—a world where understanding and addressing your clients' emotions and needs is the ultimate competitive advantage.

The Foundation of Trust and Connection

1. **Active Listening**: Your clients want to feel heard. Show genuine interest by listening without interrupting and asking thoughtful questions. Active listening not only uncovers pain points but also demonstrates care and understanding.
2. **Transparency**: Honesty builds trust. Be upfront about what your product or service can and cannot do. If a mistake occurs, own it and take corrective action promptly.
3. **Consistency**: Trust is built over time. Consistently deliver on your promises and provide a reliable experience across every interaction.
4. **Empathy in Action**: Go beyond sympathy by taking proactive steps to solve your clients' problems. Empathy isn't just about understanding; it's about taking action.

Creating Emotional Resonance

People may forget what you said or did, but they will never forget how you made them feel. Emotional resonance is the key to creating memorable experiences that deepen loyalty.

1. **Tell Relatable Stories**: Share success stories, challenges, or moments of vulnerability that align with your clients' experiences.
2. **Humanize Your Brand**: Highlight the people behind your business. Whether it's a behind-the-scenes look at your team or a heartfelt message from the founder, showing your human side fosters connection.
3. **Celebrate Milestones**: Acknowledge important events in your clients' lives—from birthdays to business anniversaries. Small gestures leave lasting impressions.

Turning Clients into Raving Fans

Satisfied clients are good, but raving fans are transformative. These are the individuals who actively promote your brand, defend it against criticism, and remain loyal through thick and thin. Here's how to cultivate them:

1. Deliver Wow Experiences

Go beyond meeting expectations; exceed them. Surprise your clients with unexpected perks, personalized thank-you notes, or exclusive offers.

Example: A SaaS company might send a handwritten note to a client who has reached a major milestone using their platform.

2. Empower and Educate

Provide resources, tutorials, or training sessions that help clients maximize the value of your product or service.

Example: A fitness brand could offer free webinars on meal planning or stress management to enhance the customer's overall well-being.

3. Build a Community

Create spaces where your clients can connect with like-minded individuals. Online forums, social media groups, or in-person events foster a sense of belonging.

Example: A photography brand might launch a Facebook group where users can share their work, exchange tips, and participate in challenges.

4. Reward Loyalty

Show appreciation for long-term clients through exclusive benefits, such as early access to products, VIP customer support, or loyalty discounts.

Example: A subscription service could offer a free month for every year a client remains subscribed.

5. Invite Feedback and Act on It

Regularly seek input from your clients and use their suggestions to improve your offerings. When clients see their feedback implemented, it reinforces their value to your business.

Example: An e-commerce store might create a "Customer Ideas" section on their website, highlighting suggestions that have been turned into new features or products.

Sustaining the Empathy Economy

Empathy isn't a one-time effort; it's an ongoing commitment. To sustain trust and connection:

1. **Stay Attuned to Evolving Needs**: Regularly reassess your clients' goals, challenges, and preferences. Use surveys, interviews, and analytics to stay informed.
2. **Train Your Team**: Ensure every team member, from sales to support, embodies empathy and understands its importance in client interactions.
3. **Lead by Example**: As a leader, demonstrate empathy in every decision and communication. Your behavior sets the tone for your entire organization.

Action Steps:

1. Identify three ways to enhance emotional resonance in your client interactions.
2. Develop a strategy to surprise and delight your top clients within the next month.
3. Create a feedback loop to gather and act on client suggestions.
4. Plan one initiative to build a community among your customers.

By prioritizing trust, connection, and empathy, you'll not only retain clients but also inspire them to become your most passionate advocates. The empathy economy isn't just a trend—it's the foundation for sustainable, long-term success.

Chapter 10: The Relentless Innovator

Staying Ahead of Market Trends and Competitors

In today's rapidly changing business landscape, innovation is not optional—it's a necessity. To remain competitive, you must anticipate market shifts, embrace new opportunities, and adapt to evolving customer needs. The relentless innovator doesn't just keep up with trends; they create them.

The Mindset of a Relentless Innovator

1. **Curiosity as a Superpower**: Innovators constantly ask, *"What if?"* and *"Why not?"* They question the status quo and seek new ways to solve problems.
2. **Agility Over Rigidity**: The ability to pivot quickly is essential. Embrace flexibility and be willing to change direction when opportunities arise.
3. **Customer-Centric Thinking**: Focus on your customers' unmet needs and aspirations. The best innovations solve problems customers didn't even know they had.
4. **Data-Driven Decision-Making**: Leverage analytics and insights to guide your strategies. Innovation isn't guesswork; it's informed creativity.

Identifying Market Trends

1. **Stay Informed**:
   - Follow industry blogs, podcasts, and thought leaders.
   - Use tools like Google Trends or social listening platforms to spot emerging patterns.
2. **Engage with Your Audience**:
   - Conduct surveys and interviews to understand your customers' evolving needs.
   - Monitor feedback on social media and review sites for insights.
3. **Analyze Competitors**:
   - Study what your competitors are doing, but don't imitate. Look for gaps they've overlooked.
   - Use SWOT analysis (Strengths, Weaknesses, Opportunities, Threats) to position yourself strategically.
4. **Collaborate Across Industries**:
   - Look outside your niche for inspiration. Cross-industry insights often lead to groundbreaking ideas.

Creating Blue Oceans in Any Industry

The concept of a "Blue Ocean Strategy" involves breaking free from cutthroat competition in "red oceans" by creating new markets and demand. Relentless innovators consistently identify opportunities to stand out and redefine their industries.

Steps to Create a Blue Ocean

1. **Identify Untapped Needs**:
   - What problems remain unsolved in your industry?
   - How can you provide value in a way that no one else is?
2. **Simplify the Complex**:
   - Innovation often lies in making the complicated simple. Can you streamline a process, product, or service?
3. **Combine and Reimagine**:
   - Combine existing ideas in unique ways. Hybrid concepts often lead to entirely new markets.
   - **Example**: Think of how Airbnb combined the hospitality industry with peer-to-peer sharing.
4. **Focus on Value Innovation**:
   - Instead of competing on price or features, focus on creating new value for customers.
   - **Example**: Tesla redefined electric cars by focusing on performance and design, not just eco-friendliness.

Building a Culture of Innovation

1. **Encourage Experimentation**:
   - Create an environment where team members feel safe to test new ideas and fail fast.
   - Celebrate lessons learned from failures as much as successes.

2. **Invest in Continuous Learning**:
    - o Provide opportunities for your team to learn new skills and stay updated on industry advancements.
    - o Host workshops, attend conferences, or bring in expert speakers.
3. **Break Down Silos**:
    - o Foster collaboration across departments to spark diverse perspectives.
    - o Cross-functional teams often generate the most innovative ideas.
4. **Incentivize Innovation**:
    - o Recognize and reward employees who contribute creative solutions.
    - o Implement a formal process for pitching and funding new ideas.

Staying Ahead of Competitors

1. **Be Proactive, Not Reactive**:
    - o Don't wait for competitors to make the first move. Lead the charge with bold initiatives.
2. **Offer an Unparalleled Experience**:
    - o Differentiate through exceptional customer experiences that your competitors can't replicate.
3. **Leverage Technology**:
    - o Stay at the forefront of technological advancements to streamline operations and enhance offerings.
    - o **Example**: Use AI to personalize customer interactions or blockchain to improve transparency.
4. **Track Key Metrics**:
    - o Regularly assess performance indicators such as market share, customer retention, and satisfaction to identify opportunities for improvement.

Action Steps:

1. Conduct a brainstorming session with your team to identify untapped customer needs.
2. Research cross-industry innovations and explore how they can be applied to your business.
3. Develop a pilot program to test one new idea with a small segment of your audience.
4. Analyze your current processes and identify one area to simplify or streamline.
5. Create a rewards system for employees who contribute innovative ideas.

By adopting the mindset and strategies of a relentless innovator, you can stay ahead of market trends, create blue oceans, and position your business as a leader in any industry. Innovation isn't just about staying relevant—it's about shaping the future.

Chapter 11: The Feedback Loop

Analyzing and Optimizing Every Step of the Process

Growth in business is not a straight line. It's a series of steps, refinements, and adjustments driven by feedback. The feedback loop is your secret weapon for continuous improvement, ensuring every part of your process is optimized for maximum impact.

The Components of an Effective Feedback Loop

1. **Input Collection**: Gather data and insights from every possible source:
    - o Customer feedback through surveys, reviews, and interviews.
    - o Analytics from your website, social media, and sales funnels.
    - o Internal team feedback on workflows and processes.
2. **Analysis and Insights**:
    - o Look for patterns in your data. What's working? What isn't?
    - o Identify bottlenecks and areas for improvement.
    - o Use tools like Google Analytics, Hotjar, or CRM dashboards to make data-driven decisions.
3. **Action and Implementation**:
    - o Develop strategies to address weaknesses and build on strengths.
    - o Assign clear ownership and deadlines for implementing changes.
4. **Measurement and Iteration**:
    - o Test changes and monitor results.
    - o Repeat the cycle to refine and perfect.

Turning Failures Into Stepping Stones for Growth

Failure is not the opposite of success; it's a vital part of the journey. The most successful businesses embrace failure as an opportunity to learn, adapt, and innovate.

The Growth Mindset

1. **Reframe Failures as Lessons**:
    - o Instead of asking, "Why did this go wrong?" ask, "What can we learn from this?"
    - o Create a culture where mistakes are seen as opportunities rather than setbacks.

2. **Analyze Root Causes**:
   o Use frameworks like the "5 Whys" to dig deep into the underlying issues.
   o Address root causes rather than surface-level symptoms.
3. **Share Lessons Across Teams**:
   o Document failures and the lessons learned.
   o Share these insights across departments to prevent similar mistakes in the future.
4. **Celebrate Effort and Progress**:
   o Recognize teams for taking risks, even if the outcome isn't perfect.
   o This encourages innovation and prevents a fear of failure.

Practical Steps to Build a Feedback Loop

Step 1: Define Key Metrics

- Identify the metrics that matter most to your business goals (e.g., conversion rates, customer satisfaction scores, retention rates).
- Regularly track and review these metrics to identify trends and anomalies.

Step 2: Establish Feedback Channels

- Use customer surveys, focus groups, and live chats to gather qualitative insights.
- Monitor online reviews and social media mentions to gauge sentiment.
- Implement employee feedback systems to understand internal challenges.

Step 3: Implement Tools for Analysis

- Analytics platforms (e.g., Google Analytics, Mixpanel) for quantitative data.
- Heatmaps (e.g., Crazy Egg, Hotjar) to understand user behavior.
- Project management tools (e.g., Trello, Asana) to track feedback implementation.

Step 4: Act on Feedback

- Prioritize changes based on impact and feasibility.
- Develop an action plan with clear objectives, timelines, and accountability.

Step 5: Monitor and Iterate

- After implementing changes, review the results.
- Iterate as needed to refine your approach and continue improving.

Real-Life Examples of Feedback in Action

1. **Customer Experience Improvements**:
   - A software company notices that users frequently abandon onboarding halfway. After analyzing feedback, they simplify the process, leading to a 30% increase in activation rates.
2. **Product Development**:
   - A fitness brand introduces a new app feature that receives mixed reviews. They gather user feedback, make adjustments, and relaunch it, resulting in a 50% improvement in user satisfaction.

3. **Internal Process Optimization**:
   - A marketing team identifies delays in content approval. By streamlining workflows and introducing a project management tool, they reduce turnaround times by 40%.

Action Steps:

1. Identify one area of your business where feedback is underutilized.
2. Set up a feedback collection process (e.g., surveys, analytics tools) for that area.
3. Analyze the data and develop a plan to address key findings.
4. Implement changes and monitor results over the next quarter.
5. Document lessons learned and share them with your team.

By creating and leveraging a robust feedback loop, you'll transform challenges into opportunities and failures into stepping stones for growth. The journey to excellence is iterative, and with each cycle, you'll move closer to achieving your goals.

Chapter 12: The Legacy of Limitless Success

How to Build a Business that Outlasts You

True success isn't measured by what you achieve in your lifetime; it's measured by what you leave behind. Building a business that outlasts you requires foresight, strategy, and a commitment to creating something greater than yourself. Legacy businesses are not just profitable; they are purpose-driven, resilient, and deeply impactful.

The Foundations of a Lasting Business

1. **Purpose Beyond Profit**:
   o Define a clear mission and vision that resonates with your audience and team.
   o Focus on solving meaningful problems and creating value for generations to come.
2. **Strong Organizational Culture**:
   o Build a culture rooted in your core values. Culture is the glue that holds your business together in challenging times.
   o Empower your team to embody these values in their decisions and actions.
3. **Scalable Systems and Processes**:
   o Develop systems that can operate effectively without your constant involvement.
   o Use technology and automation to ensure efficiency and consistency.
4. **Succession Planning**:
   o Identify and mentor future leaders within your organization.
   o Create a transition plan that ensures continuity when you step away.
5. **Sustainable Practices**:
   o Prioritize sustainability in your operations, from environmental impact to ethical sourcing.
   o A sustainable business not only survives but thrives over the long term.

Empowering Others and Sending the Elevator Back Down

Success is sweetest when it's shared. Empowering others not only enriches their lives but also amplifies your legacy. As you climb to new heights, remember to send the elevator back down to lift others up.

Ways to Empower Others

1. **Mentorship**:
   - Share your knowledge and experiences with aspiring entrepreneurs, employees, or community members.
   - Provide guidance, encouragement, and constructive feedback to help them grow.
2. **Skill Development**:
   - Invest in training and development programs for your team.
   - Encourage lifelong learning and provide resources to help them reach their full potential.
3. **Creating Opportunities**:
   - Build pathways for underrepresented groups to access opportunities within your industry.
   - Partner with organizations that align with your mission to expand your impact.
4. **Recognizing and Rewarding Contributions**:
   - Celebrate the achievements of those around you. Recognition fosters loyalty and inspires continued excellence.
   - Implement programs that share the financial success of your business, such as profit-sharing or stock options.

The Ripple Effect of Empowerment

Empowerment creates a ripple effect that extends far beyond your immediate circle. The people you uplift will, in turn, uplift others, creating a network of impact that grows exponentially. By focusing on empowerment, you turn your success into a movement, leaving a mark that endures.

Leaving a Legacy of Impact

To ensure your legacy endures, take intentional steps to solidify
your contributions:

1. **Document Your Vision**:
    o   Write down your mission, values, and long-term
        goals. This roadmap will guide your team and
        successors.
2. **Build a Trusted Advisory Board**:
    o   Assemble a diverse group of advisors who can
        provide guidance and ensure your business stays
        aligned with its purpose.
3. **Give Back to the Community**:
    o   Establish charitable initiatives or partnerships that
        align with your values.
    o   Consider creating a foundation to fund causes that
        matter to you.
4. **Celebrate Milestones and Reflect**:
    o   Regularly evaluate the progress of your business
        and its alignment with your legacy goals.
    o   Celebrate achievements and recognize the collective
        effort of your team and community.

Action Steps:

1. Write a mission statement that defines the long-term
    purpose of your business.
2. Identify one individual or group you can mentor or
    empower in the next six months.
3. Develop a plan for scaling your business's impact through
    systems, sustainability, or community initiatives.
4. Reflect on the legacy you want to leave and document the
    steps needed to achieve it.

Building a legacy of limitless success is about more than just creating wealth—it's about making a difference. By empowering others and crafting a business designed to last, you'll leave a mark that inspires future generations to dream bigger, aim higher, and achieve more.

Chapter 13: The Network Effect

Building Powerful Connections That Multiply Your Success

Success doesn't happen in isolation. It's built on the foundation of relationships, partnerships, and collaborations. The network effect is the phenomenon where the value of your business grows exponentially as your connections expand and deepen. In this chapter, you'll discover how to strategically build and nurture a high-value network that amplifies your success.

How to Build and Nurture a Network of High-Value Relationships

1. **Be Strategic in Your Approach:**
   - Identify key individuals and organizations in your industry or niche that align with your goals.
   - Attend industry events, conferences, and online forums where these connections are likely to be.
2. **Focus on Quality Over Quantity:**
   - A small, engaged network of high-value connections will drive more success than thousands of shallow relationships.
   - Build meaningful relationships by engaging in genuine, two-way conversations.
3. **Follow Up Consistently:**
   - After meeting someone, send a follow-up message to solidify the connection.
   - Schedule regular check-ins or casual catch-ups to stay on their radar.
4. **Leverage Social Media Wisely:**
   - Use LinkedIn to connect with professionals and share valuable content.
   - Engage in discussions and comment thoughtfully on posts to build visibility and credibility.
5. **Be Authentic:**
   - Approach networking with authenticity and integrity. People can sense when your intentions aren't genuine.

The Art of Giving Before Receiving: Adding Value to Others

The secret to building a powerful network is to focus on what you can give rather than what you can get. When you provide value, you establish trust, credibility, and goodwill that naturally lead to opportunities.

1. **Identify Their Needs:**
   - Pay attention to what your connections need and think about how you can help.
   - This could be sharing resources, making introductions, or offering your expertise.
2. **Be a Connector:**
   - Introduce people in your network who can benefit from knowing each other.
   - Building bridges strengthens your position as a valuable hub of connections.
3. **Share Knowledge Freely:**
   - Provide insights, advice, or recommendations without expecting anything in return.
   - Create and share content that benefits your network, such as guides, articles, or videos.
4. **Celebrate Their Success:**
   - Recognize and share their achievements on social media or within your community.
   - Celebrating others builds goodwill and strengthens relationships.

Leveraging Your Network to Create Business Opportunities, Collaborations, and Growth

1. **Collaborate on Projects:**
   - Partner with your connections on projects that align with both of your goals.
   - This could include co-hosting events, co-creating content, or launching joint ventures.
2. **Tap Into Expertise:**
   - Reach out to your network for advice, mentorship, or feedback on your ideas.
   - Leveraging their knowledge can save time and prevent costly mistakes.
3. **Open Doors to New Opportunities:**
   - Your connections can introduce you to potential clients, partners, or investors.
   - Don't hesitate to ask for introductions when it's mutually beneficial.
4. **Build a Referral Pipeline:**
   - Encourage your network to refer your products or services to their connections.
   - Offer incentives, such as discounts or commissions, to create a win-win situation.

Real-Life Examples of How Networks Amplify Success

Example 1: Airbnb's Early Boost

When Airbnb was struggling to gain traction, the founders connected with influencers in the tech and travel industries.

These early advocates helped amplify Airbnb's message, leading to rapid growth and mainstream success.

Example 2: Oprah's Endorsement of Spanx

Sara Blakely, founder of Spanx, sent a personal pitch to Oprah Winfrey, who became a fan and featured Spanx on her show. This endorsement catapulted Spanx to international fame and exponential growth.

Example 3: LinkedIn as a Career Catalyst

Many professionals have used LinkedIn not just for job hunting but to connect with mentors, partners, and collaborators. One connection often leads to many more, creating a domino effect of opportunities.

Action Steps:

1. Identify five individuals you want to connect with and research how you can add value to them.
2. Attend one networking event or participate in an online forum relevant to your industry this month.
3. Make three introductions within your network to facilitate mutually beneficial connections.
4. Create and share one piece of content that provides value to your audience.

Networking is not just about growing your business; it's about enriching your journey with the ideas, support, and collaboration of others. When done right, the network effect becomes a powerful multiplier of success, opening doors to opportunities you never imagined.

Chapter 14: The Power of Personal Branding

Becoming the Face of Your Success

In the modern business landscape, your personal brand is as important as your business brand—if not more. A strong personal brand establishes authority, builds trust, and sets you apart from the competition. It's how the world perceives you, and when done right, it can become the driving force behind your success.

Crafting a Personal Brand That Aligns with Your Business Goals

1. **Define Your Core Identity:**
   - Identify your unique strengths, values, and passions.
   - Determine what you want to be known for in your industry.
2. **Align Your Personal and Business Brands:**
   - Ensure your personal brand complements your business's mission and goals.
   - Use consistent messaging, visuals, and tone across all platforms.
3. **Create a Compelling Brand Story:**
   - Share your journey, including your struggles and triumphs, to connect emotionally with your audience.
   - Highlight your "why"—the purpose driving your work.
4. **Develop Your Unique Value Proposition (UVP):**
   - Clearly articulate what sets you apart from others in your field.
   - Focus on how you solve specific problems for your audience.

Using Social Media, Content Creation, and Public Speaking to Establish Authority

1. **Leverage Social Media:**
   - Choose platforms that align with your target audience (e.g., LinkedIn for professionals, Instagram for visual storytelling).
   - Share valuable, actionable content consistently to position yourself as an expert.

2. **Create High-Value Content:**
   - Write blogs, create videos, or launch podcasts that educate and inspire your audience.
   - Use storytelling to make complex topics relatable and engaging.
3. **Engage in Public Speaking:**
   - Speak at conferences, webinars, or industry events to showcase your expertise.
   - Use these opportunities to network and connect with like-minded professionals.
4. **Collaborate with Influencers:**
   - Partner with other thought leaders to expand your reach and credibility.
   - Co-create content or appear as a guest on their platforms.

Building Trust and Relatability with Your Audience

1. **Be Authentic:**
   - Share both your successes and challenges to show your human side.
   - Avoid trying to appeal to everyone; focus on being true to yourself.
2. **Engage With Your Community:**
   - Respond to comments, messages, and questions to build meaningful relationships.
   - Host Q&A sessions or live events to connect directly with your audience.
3. **Consistency is Key:**
   - Maintain a regular posting schedule and stay true to your brand's voice.
   - Ensure every interaction reinforces the values and mission of your brand.
4. **Showcase Testimonials and Case Studies:**
   - Highlight stories from people you've impacted to build social proof.

- o Let your audience see how your work has transformed lives or businesses.

Case Studies of Entrepreneurs Who Leveraged Personal Branding for Exponential Growth

Gary Vaynerchuk: Building a Media Empire

- Started by sharing his journey as a wine retailer through YouTube.
- Used authenticity and consistent content creation to build an audience.
- Expanded into marketing, public speaking, and publishing, creating VaynerMedia.

Sara Blakely: The Relatable Innovator

- Shared her struggles and journey as the founder of Spanx.
- Used her personal story to connect with her audience, positioning Spanx as a relatable brand.
- Became a thought leader in entrepreneurship and women's empowerment.

Richard Branson: The Adventurous Visionary

- Infused his adventurous personality into the Virgin brand.
- Leveraged public stunts, social media, and storytelling to build trust and excitement.
- Positioned himself as a disruptor, attracting loyal customers and partners.

Action Steps:

1. Write your personal brand statement: *Who you are, what you stand for, and the value you offer.*
2. Choose one social media platform and commit to sharing valuable content weekly.
3. Identify an opportunity to speak publicly or appear on a podcast in the next month.
4. Develop a content calendar to ensure consistent messaging and engagement.

Your personal brand is not just a reflection of who you are today; it's a promise of what you'll deliver tomorrow. By investing in your brand and becoming the face of your success, you'll inspire trust, build authority, and unlock limitless opportunities.

Chapter 15: Embracing AI and Future Technologies

Staying Ahead in a Rapidly Changing World

The pace of technological advancement is accelerating, reshaping industries and redefining the way businesses operate. To thrive in this environment, entrepreneurs must not only understand emerging technologies but also adapt and integrate them into their strategies. By embracing artificial intelligence (AI), automation, blockchain, Web3, and other transformative technologies, you can stay ahead of the curve and unlock unprecedented opportunities.

How AI and Automation Are Reshaping Industries and Opportunities

Key Impacts of AI and Automation:

1. **Enhanced Efficiency:**
   - AI streamlines processes, reduces manual labor, and speeds up decision-making.
   - Examples: Predictive analytics for supply chain management, automated email campaigns, and AI-driven chatbots.

2. **Data-Driven Insights:**
   - AI processes massive datasets to uncover trends, predict customer behavior, and optimize operations.
   - Example: Retailers use AI to analyze purchase patterns and recommend personalized products.

3. **Improved Customer Experience:**
   - AI enhances personalization and responsiveness, ensuring customers feel understood and valued.
   - Example: AI-powered recommendation engines on platforms like Netflix or Spotify.

4. **New Business Models:**
   - Automation enables scalable subscription services, on-demand delivery, and gig-based marketplaces.
   - Example: Uber's algorithm-powered ride-hailing platform.

Practical Ways to Integrate AI into Marketing, Operations, and Customer Experience

Marketing:

1. **Personalized Campaigns:**
   - Use AI tools like Jasper or Adobe Sensei to craft personalized ads and emails.
   - Leverage AI-driven platforms to segment audiences and predict which messages resonate most.
2. **Content Generation and Optimization:**
   - Automate blog writing, social media posts, and video editing with tools like ChatGPT or Canva.
   - Use SEO tools powered by AI, such as SEMrush or Moz, to optimize digital content.
3. **Social Media Listening:**
   - Use AI to monitor brand mentions, trends, and sentiment analysis on platforms like Hootsuite or Brandwatch.

Operations:

1. **Process Automation:**
   - Implement tools like Zapier or UiPath to automate repetitive tasks such as invoicing and data entry.
   - Use AI to manage inventory and forecast demand more accurately.
2. **Predictive Maintenance:**
   - Use sensors and AI algorithms to monitor equipment and predict failures before they occur.
3. **Workflow Optimization:**
   - AI tools like Monday.com or Trello can analyze task assignments and improve team productivity.

Customer Experience:

1. **Chatbots and Virtual Assistants:**
   - Use AI-powered assistants like Intercom or Drift for 24/7 customer support.
2. **Personalized Shopping Experiences:**
   - Deploy AI to recommend products, customize pricing, or tailor promotions based on user behavior.
3. **Voice and Image Recognition:**
   - Integrate voice assistants (like Alexa) or image recognition tools to create seamless interactions.

Understanding Blockchain, Web3, and Other Transformative Technologies

Blockchain:

- **What It Is:**
  - A decentralized ledger technology that ensures transparency, security, and traceability.
- **Applications:**
  - Smart contracts: Automating agreements without intermediaries.
  - Supply chain transparency: Tracking goods from origin to consumer.
  - Cryptocurrencies: Creating alternative payment systems and digital assets.

Web3:

- **What It Is:**
  - The next iteration of the internet, emphasizing decentralization, data ownership, and user control.

- **Opportunities:**
  - o Decentralized apps (dApps): Platforms that operate without centralized servers.
  - o Tokenized economies: Rewarding users for participation.
  - o NFT marketplaces: Creating and trading digital assets.

Additional Technologies to Watch:

1. **Internet of Things (IoT):** Connecting devices to share data and streamline operations.
2. **Augmented Reality (AR) and Virtual Reality (VR):** Transforming user experiences in retail, education, and entertainment.
3. **Quantum Computing:** Offering unparalleled computational power for complex problem-solving.

Preparing for the Future: Anticipating and Adapting to Technological Shifts

1. **Stay Informed:**
   - o Follow industry blogs, tech news, and innovation-focused podcasts.
   - o Attend conferences or webinars on emerging technologies.
2. **Invest in Training:**
   - o Upskill yourself and your team to work with AI, blockchain, and other advanced tools.
   - o Partner with tech-focused consultants or training providers.
3. **Experiment and Prototype:**
   - o Test new technologies in low-risk environments before scaling.
   - o Create pilot programs to gather data and refine your approach.

4. **Foster a Culture of Innovation:**
   - Encourage employees to explore and propose tech-driven ideas.
   - Reward experimentation and celebrate successes and lessons learned.
5. **Monitor Consumer Behavior:**
   - Pay attention to how your customers adopt new technologies.
   - Adapt your offerings to align with their preferences and expectations.

Action Steps:

1. Identify one area of your business where AI could increase efficiency or improve customer experience.
2. Research a Web3 or blockchain application relevant to your industry and explore its potential.
3. Develop a plan for ongoing education and training in emerging technologies.
4. Launch a small-scale pilot project using a new technology and measure its impact.

By embracing AI and future technologies, you'll not only stay ahead of your competitors but also create innovative solutions that resonate with the evolving needs of your customers. The future belongs to those who are willing to adapt, experiment, and lead.

Chapter 16: Mastering Emotional Intelligence

The Hidden Edge in Leadership and Business

In the fast-paced world of business, technical skills and strategy are essential, but they're not enough to ensure success. Emotional Intelligence (EQ) has emerged as a critical factor that sets exceptional leaders and businesses apart. EQ is the ability to recognize, understand, and manage emotions—both your own and those of others.

In a world driven by connection, empathy, and authenticity, mastering EQ is the hidden edge that transforms good entrepreneurs into great ones.

Why Emotional Intelligence (EQ) Is More Critical Than Ever

1. **The Human-Centric Era:**
   - Customers and employees alike value genuine, empathetic interactions.
   - EQ enables leaders to create meaningful connections, build trust, and foster loyalty.
2. **Improved Decision-Making:**
   - Leaders with high EQ can separate emotion from logic, making balanced and thoughtful decisions.
3. **Navigating Complexity:**
   - Modern business involves managing diverse teams, fast-changing environments, and unexpected challenges.
   - EQ helps entrepreneurs stay resilient, adaptable, and composed.
4. **The Competitive Advantage:**
   - EQ improves communication, collaboration, and conflict resolution, giving businesses an edge in team performance and customer relationships.

Understanding and Managing Your Own Emotions as an Entrepreneur

1. Self-Awareness:

- Recognize your emotional triggers and patterns.
- Reflect on how your emotions influence your decisions and interactions.
- Practice mindfulness to stay present and attuned to your feelings.

2. Self-Regulation:

- Develop strategies to manage stress and avoid emotional reactivity.
- Pause before responding in high-pressure situations.
- Use techniques like deep breathing, journaling, or physical activity to process emotions constructively.

3. Motivation:

- Cultivate intrinsic motivation by focusing on your mission and purpose.
- Set meaningful goals that align with your values.
- Celebrate small wins to maintain momentum and positivity.

Building Empathy and Strong Relationships with Your Team, Partners, and Customers

1. Active Listening:

- Give your full attention during conversations.
- Ask open-ended questions and validate the speaker's feelings.
- Avoid interrupting or jumping to solutions too quickly.

2. Empathy in Action:

- Put yourself in others' shoes to understand their perspectives and challenges.
- Respond with compassion and offer support tailored to their needs.

3. Strengthening Team Dynamics:

- Encourage open communication and collaboration within your team.
- Recognize and celebrate individual contributions to foster a sense of belonging.
- Address misunderstandings and tensions proactively.

4. Enhancing Customer Relationships:

- Show genuine care for your customers' experiences and outcomes.
- Use feedback to continuously improve your products and services.
- Personalize interactions to make customers feel valued.

Strategies to Handle Conflict, Inspire Loyalty, and Lead with Authenticity

Handling Conflict:

1. **Stay Calm and Objective:**
   - Avoid reacting defensively. Focus on understanding the root cause of the issue.

2. **Use Collaborative Problem-Solving:**
   - o Frame conflicts as opportunities to find mutually beneficial solutions.
3. **Maintain Respect:**
   - o Acknowledge differing viewpoints and avoid blaming or criticizing.

Inspiring Loyalty:

1. **Lead by Example:**
   - o Demonstrate the behavior and values you want to see in others.
2. **Invest in Relationships:**
   - o Show genuine interest in your team's and customers' well-being and success.
3. **Deliver on Promises:**
   - o Build trust by consistently following through on commitments.

Leading with Authenticity:

1. **Be Transparent:**
   - o Share your vision, challenges, and decisions openly with your team.
2. **Align Actions with Values:**
   - o Let your principles guide your leadership style and decision-making.
3. **Encourage Vulnerability:**
   - o Acknowledge your limitations and seek input from others to foster collaboration and trust.

Action Steps:

1. Schedule 15 minutes daily for self-reflection to identify emotional triggers and patterns.
2. Practice active listening in your next conversation by giving your full attention and asking thoughtful questions.
3. Identify one high-pressure situation and use self-regulation techniques to respond constructively.
4. Facilitate a team-building exercise that encourages open communication and empathy.

Mastering emotional intelligence is not a one-time achievement— it's a lifelong journey. By understanding and managing your own emotions, building empathetic relationships, and leading with authenticity, you'll create a ripple effect of positive impact that transforms your business and the lives of those you touch.

Chapter 17: The Global Entrepreneur

Expanding Your Business Beyond Borders

In an increasingly interconnected world, the opportunities for entrepreneurs to expand internationally are greater than ever. Taking your business beyond borders opens doors to new markets, diverse audiences, and exponential growth. However, it also presents unique challenges that require careful planning and adaptation. This chapter will guide you through the key considerations for becoming a global entrepreneur.

Opportunities and Challenges in International Markets

Opportunities:

1. **Larger Customer Base:**
   - Access to a global audience increases your potential for revenue and brand visibility.
   - Example: A niche product in your home country might have massive demand in another region.
2. **Diversification:**
   - Expanding into multiple markets reduces dependence on one economy.
   - Example: If one country experiences a downturn, others can sustain your business.
3. **Competitive Edge:**
   - Establishing a global presence can set you apart from competitors who remain local.
4. **Innovation Through Diversity:**
   - Exposure to different cultures and markets sparks fresh ideas and product innovations.

Challenges:

1. **Cultural Differences:**
   - Misunderstanding local customs, traditions, or consumer behavior can hinder success.
2. **Regulatory Barriers:**
   - Navigating complex laws, taxes, and trade regulations in each country.
3. **Logistics and Operations:**
   - Managing shipping, inventory, and customer support across borders.
4. **Market Saturation:**
   - Competing with established local businesses and adapting to pricing structures.

Adapting Your Products, Services, and Messaging for Different Cultures

1. **Conduct Market Research:**
   - Understand the preferences, buying habits, and pain points of your target audience in each region.
   - Use surveys, focus groups, and local market data to inform your strategy.
2. **Localize Your Offerings:**
   - Adapt your products and services to meet local tastes and needs.
   - Example: McDonald's customizes its menu in India with vegetarian options and spices.
3. **Tailor Your Messaging:**
   - Translate marketing materials accurately and ensure cultural relevance.
   - Avoid literal translations that may lead to misunderstandings.
   - Example: Coca-Cola's slogan "Taste the Feeling" is adapted into emotional equivalents in different languages.
4. **Engage Local Talent:**
   - Partner with local marketers, translators, and advisors who understand the culture.

Navigating Global Regulations and Logistics

1. **Understand Trade Regulations:**
   - Research import/export restrictions, tariffs, and trade agreements.
   - Partner with legal experts or consultants specializing in international trade.

2. **Tax Compliance:**
   - Register your business for international tax obligations, such as VAT or GST.
   - Use software like Avalara or hire accountants with global expertise.
3. **Shipping and Fulfillment:**
   - Partner with reliable logistics providers like DHL, FedEx, or local couriers.
   - Offer transparent shipping costs and timelines to customers.
4. **Payment Systems:**
   - Integrate global payment platforms like PayPal, Stripe, or Wise.
   - Offer local payment options preferred in specific regions (e.g., Alipay in China).
5. **Customer Support:**
   - Provide multilingual support via chatbots, email, or call centers.
   - Train your team to address cultural nuances in customer interactions.

Leveraging Digital Tools to Reach Customers Worldwide

1. **E-Commerce Platforms:**
   - Use platforms like Shopify, WooCommerce, or Amazon to sell globally.
   - Enable features like currency conversion and international shipping.
2. **Social Media Marketing:**
   - Leverage region-specific platforms (e.g., WeChat in China, VKontakte in Russia).
   - Create geo-targeted ads to reach specific demographics.

3. **SEO and Localization:**
   - Optimize your website for local search engines (e.g., Baidu for China, Yandex for Russia).
   - Use region-specific keywords and metadata.
4. **Analytics and Insights:**
   - Track global performance using tools like Google Analytics or HubSpot.
   - Monitor KPIs such as traffic by country, conversion rates, and customer retention.
5. **Digital Communication Tools:**
   - Use Zoom, Microsoft Teams, or Slack to collaborate with international teams.
   - Schedule meetings that accommodate time zone differences.

Action Steps:

1. Identify one international market with strong potential for your product or service.
2. Conduct market research to understand cultural and regulatory nuances.
3. Develop a localized marketing plan, including translated materials and region-specific campaigns.
4. Partner with a logistics provider to establish reliable international shipping.
5. Set up global payment options and test your e-commerce platform for seamless cross-border transactions.

Expanding your business beyond borders requires a mix of curiosity, adaptability, and strategy. By embracing cultural diversity, navigating regulations, and leveraging digital tools, you can unlock the immense potential of international markets and position yourself as a truly global entrepreneur.

Chapter 18: Resilience in the Face of Uncertainty

Thriving When the Unexpected Happens

Uncertainty is an inevitable part of the entrepreneurial journey. From economic downturns to industry disruptions, unexpected challenges can threaten the stability of even the most well-established businesses. However, resilience—the ability to adapt and thrive in the face of adversity—is what separates those who survive from those who succeed.

This chapter explores practical strategies for navigating uncertainty, creating contingency plans, and turning challenges into opportunities.

Strategies for Navigating Economic Downturns, Market Shifts, and Crises

1. Stay Informed and Anticipate Change

- Monitor industry trends, economic indicators, and competitor activity to identify potential risks and opportunities.
- Engage with thought leaders and industry groups to gain diverse perspectives on emerging challenges.

2. Prioritize Cash Flow Management

- Maintain a cash reserve to weather periods of reduced revenue.
- Review expenses regularly and eliminate unnecessary costs.
- Negotiate flexible payment terms with suppliers and explore financing options.

3. Diversify Revenue Streams

- Expand your offerings to serve multiple markets or customer segments.
- Introduce subscription models, partnerships, or complementary products.
- Example: A restaurant that added meal delivery and virtual cooking classes during the pandemic.

4. Maintain Open Communication

- Be transparent with employees, partners, and customers about challenges and plans.
- Build trust by providing regular updates and involving key stakeholders in decision-making.

5. Invest in Technology

- Leverage digital tools to increase efficiency, automate processes, and reach new audiences.
- Example: Retailers that adopted e-commerce platforms to sustain sales during lockdowns.

The Importance of a Contingency Plan and Agile Thinking

1. What Is a Contingency Plan?

- A contingency plan outlines actions to take when unexpected events disrupt normal operations.
- It provides a clear roadmap for mitigating risks, ensuring continuity, and minimizing damage.

2. Key Elements of a Contingency Plan

- **Risk Assessment:** Identify potential threats and their impact on your business.
- **Critical Operations:** Determine which processes and resources are essential to sustain operations.
- **Action Steps:** Outline specific measures for responding to different scenarios.
- **Communication Protocols:** Define how and when to communicate with stakeholders.

- **Testing and Review:** Regularly test your plan and update it based on lessons learned.

3. Agile Thinking in Practice

- Embrace flexibility by being open to new ideas, approaches, and solutions.
- Empower your team to make quick decisions and adapt to changing circumstances.
- Example: A software company that shifted its product roadmap to prioritize remote work solutions during COVID-19.

Turning Adversity into Opportunity

1. Reframe Challenges as Opportunities

- View obstacles as a chance to innovate, improve, and differentiate your business.
- Ask, "What can we learn from this?" and "How can we emerge stronger?"
- **2. Focus on Core Strengths**

- Double down on what your business does best and find ways to amplify its value.
- Example: A fitness brand that pivoted to online classes during gym closures.

3. Listen to Your Customers

- Engage with your audience to understand their evolving needs and preferences.
- Use this feedback to develop solutions that address their pain points.

4. Inspiring Stories of Resilience

- **Airbnb:** Faced with mass cancellations during the pandemic, Airbnb pivoted to offering virtual experiences and long-term rentals, keeping the business afloat and diversifying its offerings.
- **LEGO:** During a financial crisis, LEGO refocused on its core product and introduced innovative sets, including partnerships with franchises like Star Wars, leading to a significant turnaround.
- **Zoom:** When remote work surged, Zoom scaled its infrastructure rapidly and offered free services to schools, solidifying its position as a market leader.

Action Steps:

1. Conduct a risk assessment to identify potential vulnerabilities in your business.
2. Develop a contingency plan that addresses your most critical operations.
3. Identify one area where you can innovate or diversify your offerings in response to current challenges.
4. Schedule a brainstorming session with your team to explore ways to turn adversity into opportunity.
5. Share an inspiring story of resilience with your team to reinforce a culture of adaptability and optimism.

Resilience is not about avoiding challenges—it's about navigating them with clarity, confidence, and creativity. By preparing for the unexpected and maintaining an agile mindset, you can transform uncertainty into a catalyst for growth and innovation, ensuring your business thrives in any environment.

Bonus: The Epic Case Studies

Real Stories of Businesses That Went from Zero to Millions

Success leaves clues and studying the journeys of trailblazing businesses can offer invaluable lessons for your own growth.

These epic case studies highlight real-world examples of entrepreneurs who overcame challenges, seized opportunities, and built empires from the ground up.

Case Study 1: The Digital Disruptor

Company: Dollar Shave Club
Industry: Subscription-Based E-Commerce
Revenue Milestone: $1 Billion Acquisition by Unilever

The Challenge:

Traditional razor companies dominated the market, making it nearly impossible for small players to compete. Consumers were frustrated with high prices and complicated product offerings.

The Strategy:

1. **Unique Positioning:**
   o Focused on affordability and convenience with a $1/month subscription model.
2. **Viral Marketing:**
   o Released a humorous, no-frills video ad that resonated with a broad audience, amassing millions of views.
3. **Customer-Centric Approach:**
   o Simplified product selection and emphasized ease of delivery.

Key Takeaway:

Creativity and customer-focused innovation can level the playing field against industry giants.

Case Study 2: The Underdog Innovator

Company: Spanx
Industry: Apparel
Revenue Milestone: $400+ Million in Annual Sales

The Challenge:

Sara Blakely, the founder of Spanx, had no background in fashion or retail and faced resistance from manufacturers and retailers.

The Strategy:

1. **Bootstrapping:**
   o Used $5,000 in savings to develop the product, skipping external funding.
2. **Relentless Sales Effort:**
   o Personally pitched the product to retailers and demonstrated its unique value.
3. **Influencer Endorsement:**
   o Oprah Winfrey's public endorsement propelled Spanx into the spotlight.

Key Takeaway:

Passion and persistence can overcome industry barriers and lack of experience.

Case Study 3: The Community Builder

Company: Patagonia
Industry: Outdoor Apparel
Revenue Milestone: $1 Billion in Annual Sales

The Challenge:

The outdoor apparel market was saturated, and customers were increasingly concerned about environmental impact.

The Strategy:

1. **Sustainability Commitment:**
   o   Adopted eco-friendly practices and promoted sustainability as a core value.
2. **Community Engagement:**
   o   Built a loyal customer base by aligning with causes their audience cared about.
3. **Transparency:**
   o   Shared detailed information about their supply chain and environmental efforts.

Key Takeaway:

A strong mission and community alignment create lifelong brand loyalty.

Case Study 4: The Tech Visionary

Company: Airbnb
Industry: Hospitality and Travel
Revenue Milestone: $8.4 Billion Annual Revenue (2022)

The Challenge:

Breaking into the hospitality industry dominated by hotels while convincing strangers to share their homes.

The Strategy:

1. **Platform Trust:**
   o Implemented review systems and identity verification to build trust between hosts and guests.
2. **Scalable Model:**
   o Focused on creating a peer-to-peer platform that scaled without owning physical inventory.
3. **Local Experiences:**
   o Highlighted unique, local experiences unavailable through traditional hotels.

Key Takeaway:

Solving trust issues and leveraging underutilized assets can create entirely new markets.

Case Study 5: The Social Media Maven

Company: Glossier
Industry: Beauty and Skincare
Revenue Milestone: $100 Million in Annual Sales

The Challenge:

Competing with established beauty brands with massive budgets.

The Strategy:

1. **Direct-to-Consumer (DTC):**
   o Sold exclusively through their website, bypassing traditional retail.
2. **Social Media Engagement:**
   o Built a devoted community by encouraging user-generated content and showcasing real customers.

3. **Product Simplicity:**
    o Focused on a curated range of products rather than overwhelming consumers with options.

Key Takeaway:

Authenticity and community engagement can outperform traditional advertising.

Common Threads Among These Case Studies

1. **Customer Obsession:**
    o Every business focused intently on solving specific customer pain points.
2. **Creativity Over Resources:**
    o Founders leveraged creativity, resourcefulness, and grit to overcome financial and logistical challenges.
3. **Mission-Driven:**
    o Strong alignment with a clear purpose fostered brand loyalty and differentiation.
4. **Bold Marketing:**
    o Whether through viral videos or grassroots efforts, each company made bold moves to capture attention.

Action Steps:

1. Identify one lesson from these case studies that aligns with your business goals.
2. Brainstorm how you can creatively solve a customer pain point in your industry.
3. Write a one-paragraph mission statement that clearly articulates your purpose.
4. Develop a marketing plan that highlights your unique value proposition.

These epic case studies prove that success isn't reserved for the privileged few. With innovation, persistence, and a customer-first mindset, you too can go from zero to millions.

Conclusion: Your Next Chapter

A Call to Action for Limitless Growth

You've reached the end of this book, but your journey is only the beginning. The lessons, strategies, and tools you've discovered here are not just ideas—they are stepping stones to a future filled with possibilities. Now, it's time to take action.

Success isn't about knowing what to do; it's about doing what you know. The path to limitless growth lies in your ability to turn these insights into action, one step at a time. Whether you're starting from scratch or scaling an existing business, remember that the greatest transformations happen when you consistently move forward, no matter how small the step.

Your Journey Forward

1. **Dream Big, Act Boldly**:
   o Reflect on your vision and set ambitious yet attainable goals. Don't let fear hold you back from thinking beyond limits.
2. **Leverage What You've Learned**:
   o Revisit the chapters, worksheets, and tools to refine your strategies. Use them as your playbook for navigating challenges and seizing opportunities.
3. **Stay Relentless**:
   o Challenges will come, and failures may arise. Treat them as fuel for growth, not roadblocks. Your ability to persevere will define your success.
4. **Empower Others Along the Way**:
   o Share your knowledge, mentor others, and build a legacy that inspires. True success multiplies when it's shared.

Your First Action Step

Right now, before the momentum fades, commit to one action. Choose a goal, break it into a manageable task, and take the first step today. The smallest action can spark the greatest change.

The Final Thought

You have the tools. You have the vision. Most importantly, you have the drive. Remember, growth is not a destination; it's a journey. Each step you take will bring you closer to the success you envision. Stay focused, stay inspired, and above all, stay limitless.

The future is yours to create. Go out and make it extraordinary.

Acknowledgments

This book would not have been possible without the unwavering support and encouragement of so many incredible individuals. I extend my deepest gratitude to my family, friends, and mentors, whose belief in me has been a constant source of inspiration. Your guidance and love have fueled my determination and passion every step of the way.

To the readers who have chosen to embark on this journey, thank you for trusting me to be a part of your path to success. Your dreams are the driving force behind my mission, and it is my deepest hope that this book empowers you to unlock your true potential and sell beyond limits.

Copyright Notice

Disclaimer

Sell Beyond Limits: "Dominate Any Market and Achieve Unstoppable Growth" is a copyrighted work of non-fiction. Names, characters, businesses, organizations, places, events, and incidents mentioned in this publication are either the product of the author's imagination or used fictitiously. Any resemblance to actual persons, living or deceased, events, or locales is purely coincidental.

This book is for informational and educational purposes only. It does not constitute financial, investment, or legal advice. Readers are encouraged to do their own research (DYOR) and consult with professionals before making any financial or investment decisions. The author and publisher are not liable for any outcomes resulting from actions taken based on the content of this book.

Made in the USA
Columbia, SC
09 February 2025

53469827R00063